THE DISSOLUTION OF BUILDINGS
Angelo Bucci

ANGELO BUCCI AND THE PAULISTA MODERN HOUSE
Kenneth Frampton

INTRODUCTION BY AMALE ANDRAOS

COLUMBIA BOOKS ON ARCHITECTURE
AND THE CITY, 2015

The GSAPP Transcripts series is a curated record of the major events that take place at the Columbia University Graduate School of Architecture, Planning and Preservation. Embracing the simple idea that publication is the act of making something public, these books form a channel through which the discourse internal to the school enters the public arena of architectural media and ideas, in the form of edited talks and symposia. In each case, the original lectures and discussions at the core of these books are augmented with supplementary material, additional imagery, and critical commentary, expanding their debates and provocations beyond the confines of the lecture hall.

"Architecture is an art that negotiates place and time to present to us new possibilities of being in the world."

INTRODUCTION
Amale Andraos

There are few pleasures today as meaningful as the possibility of an architecture deeply embedded within its context. This type of architecture resists cultural clichés, easy signifiers of difference, or spectacular resolutions of constructed oppositions such as local and global, or tradition and modernity. Rather, it reinvents its context, registers the ground it is built out of, and renders in almost subliminal ways a visceral understanding of its history—cultural, material, technological, and environmental. Angelo Bucci's work does just this: It weaves together past and future, site and story, grounding and lightness, the here and the there. To render the new ground it constructs an "international meeting point" for architecture and for culture at large.

This collected body of work comes on the occasion of the fourth annual Kenneth Frampton Endowed Lecture, which has come to form a rhythm of the experience of the school, as a strong moment of reflection about architecture in its most essential form, at once powerful and poetic, urgently relevant and timeless. The lectures have come to draw the widest and most diverse audience, a testimony to Kenneth Frampton as a figure whose presence, not only for Columbia but for the world at large, remains fundamental. With his eternal youth, legendary energy, endless curiosity, and rare intellectual generosity, Kenneth Frampton continues to embody what the architect as critic and writer can be at its best. His influence continues to resonate today, sending wavebands across the globe which come back to him, and to us, in the form of exquisite architecture.

And so it is always with great pleasure that each year we rediscover with Kenneth Frampton what architecture can be. Architecture is an art that negotiates place and time to present to us new possibilities of being in the world. This negotiation is one that Angelo Bucci's buildings master beautifully with care, skill, and sensitivity as they move beyond reductive notions of context to offer us, instead, an architecture at once deeply local and global. And it is a process that echoes, in the form of building, the power of Kenneth Frampton's writing.

"I believe the most challenging task in our activity as architects is not to overcome what we do not know, but conversely, to be free of what we know very well, to overcome the knowledge we inherit."

ON GROUND: THE KENNETH FRAMPTON ENDOWED LECTURE
Angelo Bucci

Angelo Bucci at Columbia University Graduate School of Architecture, Planning and Preservation, November 12, 2014.

A HOUSE IN UBATUBA

Architecture begins on the ground. A building is the product not just of the city or of the town in which it is sited—and in my case this has almost always been São Paulo—but also of the very topography on which it lies. Like a spaceship or a cave, a building alights upon or is embedded in the ground, not an imposition but rather a negotiation with its site.

Ubatuba is a coastal city on the Tropic of Capricorn, about three hours from São Paulo. In 2005 we designed a → fig. 001
house there. What we found most challenging about this project was creating a strategy to build on such a steep site with minimal environmental impact. In order to preserve the topography and the existing trees, we avoided removing, infilling, or redistributing any earth. But the grade of the site is almost 50 percent, with the street at the top, 30 meters above the beach below. The risks of building on this kind of topography in one of the rainiest sites in our tropical country were real—landslides are commonplace on the Paulista coast.

The strategy was to touch the ground on just three points, so the house rests on three columns. While the casting of → figs. 002 & 003
concrete takes place from the bottom to the top, the structure works from the top to the bottom: Two beams follow the rooftop and all three slabs hang from them. As the beams were the last piece to be cast, the structure was only stable when it was complete.

Angelo Bucci

By being hung, the slabs could be detached from
columns. In the beginning, I thought about
Alexander Calder. Considering this structure
could be balanced almost as a mobile, I thought
the slabs could be arranged to counterweigh
each other in suspension over the site. The
structural engineer, Ibsen Puleo Uvo, proved my
assumption naïve—in a static structure, perfect
balancing is not required. In general, we talk
to the structural engineer in the beginning of
the design process, as he is the man who makes
architecture come true.

Although the two tallest columns are about 10
meters high before they meet the lower slab,
they disappear among trees if we look at the
house from the beach. The slabs appear to float
on the top of the trees, and the horizontal
and vertical position of slabs provides views
to the beach from each room in the
house. Because the house serves as   → fig. 004
home for its owners as well as a
weekend house for their son and daughter, its
program is divided into parts. We split bedrooms into two separate blocks so that it is
like two or three houses that meet
in the living area.   → fig. 005

Outside and inside spaces alternate throughout
the house. These interior and exterior rooms
open onto one another and intersect
in the living space. It is a simple   → fig. 006
architectural strategy, one that is
quite appropriate for a tropical country. But
in order to be able to design that, we had to
learn how to be free from some strong cultural
inheritances from the European tradition. For

instance, while avoiding the segregation of inside and outside makes sense in the Brazilian climate, the move requires an effort to escape a cultural and architectural legacy based in European modernism.

There are two previous projects among our early works that should be mentioned here: the psychology clinic in Orlandia and the house in Ribeirão Preto. Both of these projects demonstrate the cumulative process through which our design thinking matured and evolved, moving from the references and inheritances of our education to an approach that is uniquely of this city and that responds to its urban and natural conditions.

The psychology clinic was, for me, a lesson in how to design a building through only a few deliberate actions. This was an architectural strategy that came in response to building in Orlandia, my hometown. Due to the distance between Orlandia and São Paulo, it was not possible to visit the construction site so often. Now it is clear how distance has trained me to articulate a design with the parameters of construction more clearly in mind, and it has made me more aware of issues of construction in certain ways. At that time we didn't use the computer in our office, and all blueprints were mailed directly to the workers, so the drawings were literally addressed to the mason, carpenters, and so on. The limited back-and-forth pushed us past ambiguous design decisions and allowed us to enhance those jobs in which workers had already demonstrated their skills.

We also examined this notion of distance con-
ceptually: What is the distance between inside
and outside? It could be just a door. This
project explores this boundary by expanding the
distance between the middle of the street and
the very private room of the psychoanalyst,
which is really the only indoor space. All
other rooms are not exactly inside
or outside.   → fig. 007

The house in Ribeirão Preto was one of the
first projects I designed with Ibsen Puleo Uvo.
Designing this house with him was integral in
my approach to the Ubatuba House some years
later. Both structures have the same principle,
but if we compare them, this first one is much
simpler and safer to build than the second.

The initial concept for this project came
from an adversity. The site topography used
to have, naturally, about a 10 percent slope,
but was leveled for no apparent reason other
than an absurd belief that a flat site could
make a better sale. Therefore, we had 225 cubic
meters of soil spread out without any reason.
I couldn't just lay a house on it, but I also
wanted to prevent any volume of soil removal.
Ultimately, we proposed three big boxes—concrete retaining walls that would accommodate
all of the displaced soil as monumental stones
or elevated gardens.

The structural scheme came after this initial
action on the site. In order to make the vertical distances as short as possible the first
slab has no beams. Instead, the beams were
placed on the rooftop and the floor slabs below

are suspended from them. Just two beams are
displayed at the longitudinal axis, identical
in dimension and length but not in loads. While
one is loaded the whole length, the second
crosses over the patio, free of load for most
of its span apart from its cantilevered ends.
The problem for the structural engineer was
to counterweigh the edge of those cantilevers
in order to control deformation. Initially, we
had the water tank, as usually we do in Brazil, placed at the top of a column so as to not
impose any unnecessary load to the structure—an
obvious and easy solution, we agreed. But in
the interest of balance, we placed the water
tank at the middle of the span in the beam
relieving the structure, enhancing the control
over its deformation. Although a building
is a static structure we can think
of it as a dynamic one, like   → fig. 008
Calder's mobiles.

A WEEKEND HOUSE

Reconsidering the figure of the water tank in
the house in Ribeirão Preto, appropriated in
that case as a structural component, allowed us
to explore other identities of water in later
projects. More recently, in a weekend house in
São Paulo, we thought of water as a
kind of ground.   → fig. 009

Clouds, drizzle, rain, snow, or hail—in all
its physical states, water relates to the sky.
However, if we are asked to think about a pool,
our imagination automatically starts to dig
into the ground. Seas, lakes, and ponds all

invoke water that rests smoothly on the ground.
Water defines the surface. But if I mention a
specific type of pool, a water tank, or a water
tower, we see an elevated volume of water, a
pool detached from the ground level.

In this case, the water's elevation is neces-
sary: Hydrostatic pressure is required to feed
pipes, to supply water. Water level holds a
potential possibility.

While walking on the ground, we could ask:
Where is the surface? In the specific sense of
the word, surface has no layers or thickness.
However, if one walks in a city like São Paulo
(or New York) the ground level does not correspond to the surface anymore. There are some
pieces of the ground that haven't been touched
by the sunlight for decades since buildings
have permanently shaded them.

In this specific site, the neighborhood's aver-
age height is defined by the zoning code as
6 meters high. No side setbacks are required.
The neighboring building to the east shades
our site until noon, when the building west
of us starts to shade it for the whole after-
noon. Therefore, if there is a pool to be
built, exposed to the sunlight the whole day,
it is crucial to redefine its surface at 6
meters above the ground level. To swim in a
water tower is to enjoy the potential of this
urban fixture as a design possibility; it
becomes another state of water under the sky
of São Paulo.

The roof superstructure from which the house is suspended is treated as a landscape within the landscape.
Angelo Bucci, SPBR Arquitetos, House in Ubatuba, Brazil, 2010.

The cylindrical central column supporting the roof superstructure serves as the cove for the spiral access.
Angelo Bucci, SPBR Arquitetos, House in Ubatuba, Brazil, 2010.

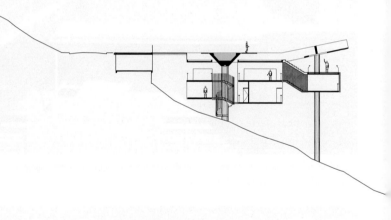

Angelo Bucci, SPBR Arquitetos, House in Ubatuba, Brazil, 2010, section drawing.

0   5   10   20m

Angelo Bucci, SPBR Arquitetos, House in Ubatuba, Brazil, 2010, veranda.

Angelo Bucci, SPBR Arquitetos, House in Ubatuba, Brazil, 2010, interior.

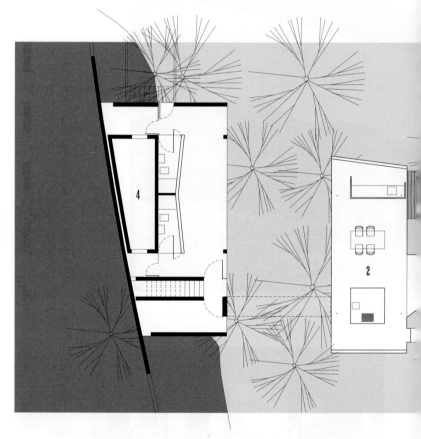

1. Living Room
2. Services
3. Veranda
4. Level

Angelo Bucci, SPBR Arquitetos, House in Ubatuba, Brazil, 2010, plan.

0 1   5m

Angelo Bucci, Psychology Clinic in Orlandia, Brazil, 1990, on the left and MMBB, House in Ribeirão, Brazil, 2001, on the right. These two works exemplify Bucci's exceptional versatile use of in situ reinforced concrete construction.

Angelo Bucci, SPBR Arquitetos, Weekend House in São Paulo, Brazil, 2012, view of the elevated swimming pool on left with the patio-garden at the lowest level on the right.

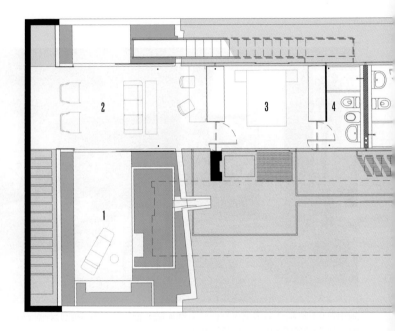

1. Terrace
2. Living Room
3. Bedroom
4. Bathroom
5. Kitchen

Angelo Bucci, SPBR Arquitetos, Weekend House in São Paulo, Brazil, 2012, second level plan drawing.

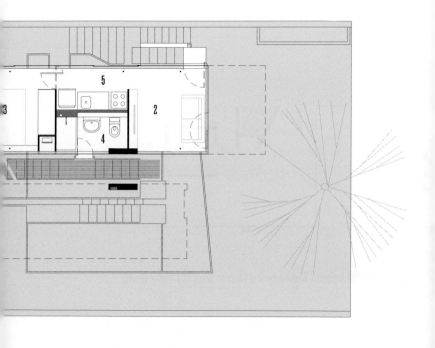

3   5   2   4

0   1   2   5m

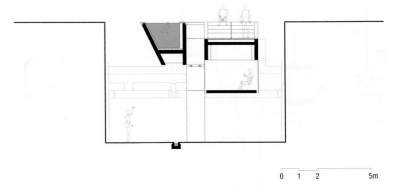

0
1
2

0 1 2   5m

Angelo Bucci, SPBR Arquitetos, Weekend House in São Paulo, Brazil, 2012, section drawing.

Angelo Bucci, SPBR Arquitetos, Weekend House in São Paulo, Brazil, 2012, circulation between pool and garden.

The ground level of the house treated as a botanical garden. Angelo Bucci, SPBR Arquitetos, Weekend House in São Paulo, Brazil, 2010.

This weekend house also responds to the conges-
tion of the city. São Paulo is a metropolis of
twenty million people, located approximately
one hour from the coast. Because of severe
traffic jams, its inhabitants spend hours com-
muting every day. On weekends, especially in
the summer, hundreds of thousands drive to the
beach causing jams on those roads as well.

In order to avoid being stuck in traffic
during weekends, we received an unexpected but
rather logical demand to design against the
flow of traffic, by building a weekend house
in downtown São Paulo. The site is very central, between an arterial avenue, Faria Lima,
and a road and railway line on the Pinheiros
river shore.

Taking an anti-floor area ratio (FAR) approach,
a swimming pool, a solarium, and
a garden are the main elements   ← fig. 010
of this project. In a properly
inverted hierarchy, all other programmatic
elements are complementary—a bedroom, a small
apartment for a caretaker, and
a space to cook and to receive   ← fig. 011
friends. The pool and solarium are
oriented as parallel volumes, with two columns
located in the 1-meter-wide gap between them.
On one side of the 12-meter span, beams support the pool, and on the other, beams support
the solarium and the floor hung underneath it.
Structurally, the mass of the pool counterbal-
ances the volume that holds inhabited spaces.
In other words, water is balanced
by the beach.   ← fig. 012

This building and its program differs from the focus of traditional architectural projects in two ways: The metropolis becomes a possible place to stay and enjoy during the weekends, and elements generally considered secondary or complementary in a typical house—swimming pool and garden—become its central figures. This second condition was the most challenging for us. How could we suppress the core of the house, the primary function of dwelling, and prevent the remaining program from fading away into gloom? How do we support "extroverted" activities without "infrastructural" program? By moving up from the introspective space of the garden on the ground level, through the private space of the apartment at the first floor, and finally to the extroverted rooftop with panoramas of the city, we modulated the moods of that house, and we made a swimming pool as if dug into the air—a pool with no ground. ← figs. 013 & 014

FAU USP: A PAULISTA SCHOOL

I want to turn now from the work I have done with my practice, to the milieu in which I was trained—what is called the Paulista School. While this well-circulated expression describes a group to which I belong, the architecture which is usually associated with the name Paulista was not a matter of consensus for us. For this reason, it is hard to identify ourselves with the label. I would like to take the opportunity to split the expression, isolating its two component words in order to refer to two distinct targets: Paulista, which refers to the

urban context of São Paulo, and School, specifically figured by the Universidade de São
Paulo Faculdade de Arquitetura e Urbanismo (FAU
USP), designed and helmed by Vilanova Artigas.
In this sense the expression becomes meaningful
to me because I consider both institutions—the
city and the school—crucial in my education as
an architect. That building and its city were
also my professors.

The FAU USP building was inaugurated in 1969.
Its designer Vilanova Artigas was also one of
the founders of the school twenty years before
in 1949. The building could be described by
stressing one of its more important features:
It is doorless. I mean, it is not a regular
building absent of doors, it is a building
whose doorlessness was a kind of first assumption of its design.

This aspect of the design marks a key departure from the architectural repertoire we have
inherited from the European tradition. For
this reason I believe the most challenging task
in our activity as architects is not to overcome what we do not know, but conversely, to
be free of what we know very well, to overcome the knowledge we inherit that so often
makes a designer act automatically or without
reflection.

The doorless FAU USP is remarkable in its
implicit provision of free and open access,
particularly in Brazil where one of the most
challenging issues is social inequality. This
building stands as a kind of monument to
this Paulista legacy, but for more than the

veneration of some remarkable professors. In true Grecian fashion, the history of the school of architecture was marked from the beginning by tragedy. Just one month after its inauguration, under the military dictatorship, Vilanova Artigas was persecuted and expelled from the school. Vilanova Artigas would be back twelve years later, in 1981, unfortunately for a very short period before his death in 1985. Even after the political situation changed, the fact he and some other professors had been brought back didn't mean the damages produced during those years had been overcome. Amnesty aside, the power force installed at the university during the dictatorship would last for decades after that.

Two other remarkable Paulista professors must be considered alongside Artigas. Flávio Motta comes out of architecture's philosophical tradition, having studied pedagogy while practicing as an artist. The second is Paulo Mendes da Rocha, one of the most significant and world-renown Brazilian architects. These Paulista figures were certainly role models, but we didn't follow them without question. Instead, the work and lives of the Paulistas before us have broadened possibilities for upcoming generations, providing fertile ground for our own experimentation.

The school seemed to transcend its faculty though. The institution provided the important foundation for our architectural education. The pedagogy was not one that dictated rules, but provided clear and practical support for an imaginative design process. I mean, literally,

the 2.75-meter ceiling grid works as a ruler. I
still know the dimensions by heart: 110 meters
long and 66 meters wide; columns every 22
meters or 11 meters; floor-to-ceiling distances
at 3.40 meters, 5.40 meters, 7.40 meters, 13
meters, or 16.80 meters. The building is itself
a device that allowed us to test scales, to
calibrate a design proposal through the infrastructure of the architectural institution.

Vilanova Artigas, Faculdade de Arquitetura e Urbanismo da Universidade de São Paulo FAU
USP, São Paulo, Brazil, 1969, student demonstration in the Central Hall of the FAU USP.

Although I never had Vilanova Artigas as my
professor at FAU USP, after experiencing that
building for so long, more and more I feel
as if I had. I believe he was so successful

instilling in the building a human value that
his students, the building's students, really
feel that architecture can embody a kind of
personality. The building was another professor
who spoke to you, sometimes emphatically in
a loud and clear voice, sometimes repeating
patiently those lessons inscribed in our minds,
sometimes kindly whispering the secrets of
someone who has learned from designing every
single day over the course of a whole life.
It is a beautiful thought that in a time when
citizens of São Paulo were silenced, the
building itself could keep talking. This is
how important an institution can be, that a
school and its essential ideas could overcome
political oppression.

Of course, it is the vitality of the community
that breathes life into institutions. During
my time at the school, it was my peers such as
Alvaro Puntoni, Alvaro Razuk, Milton Braga, and
many other colleagues who, through our everyday
interactions, instilled meaningful ideas about
architecture. Bringing people together, sharing
a same space and interest for five years, is
the treasure about the idea of a school. It is
quite obvious after some years, maybe not so
evident when one starts a school.

SÃO PAULO: A PAULISTA CITY

In the same way that a single building can
teach a student of architecture, the experience
of the city can shape the way we think about
architecture. From a very small village,
Orlandia, to the metropolitan São Paulo was

a quite shocking change: a town of twenty thousand people to a city of twenty million people,
exactly a thousand times bigger. Therefore, and
since that time, maybe due to the impact of
that change it became important to me to understand or formulate how the history of São Paulo
has forged a local culture of construction. A
key point for that understanding was to consider how the geography of the city was taken
as a foundational construction premise.

São Paulo has two clear constituent elements:
one geographical figure, which is a valley;
one piece of construction, which is a bridge.
Specifically they would be Anhangabaú Valley,
as the foundational geography, and Chá Bridge,
as the fundamental construction.

Viaduto do Chá, São Paulo, Brazil.

Angelo Bucci

Although quite specific, that elemental pair
is replicated many times over in the city
with its hundreds of rivers. It is possible to
unfold this duality in two machines, railroad
and elevator; two corresponding constructions,
bridge and high-rise buildings; two typical
programs, public and private, all spread in a
continuous horizontal plane and a vertical dis-
continuous axes. It was just a starting point
in order to recover the meaning of the activity
of architecture.

If I had to describe a unique feature of São
Paulo it would be the thickness of its ground,
20 meters. It is the distance between the
plateau, which defines the upper city level
at 745 meters high, and the riverbank, which
marks the lower city level at 725 meters. It
is entirely comprised inside that thickness,
to be precise, in the relationship between
lower and upper level and the way they merge
and blur, where I believe the architect can
most effectively operate.

A NEW MAM

Our proposal for a New Modern Art Museum, MAM,
in São Paulo is a kind of theoretical project.
It came from an invitation from Lisette Lagnado
and Ana Maria Maia, cocurators for the 33° Panorama Art Exhibition which took place at MAM in
2013. The curators presented a group of twenty-
five artists and seven architects (Andrade
Morettin, SPBR, GrupoSP, SUBdV, Y-Arquitectura,
Tacoa e Usina) with the question:
"A New MAM: Why and For Whom?"   → figs. 015 & 016

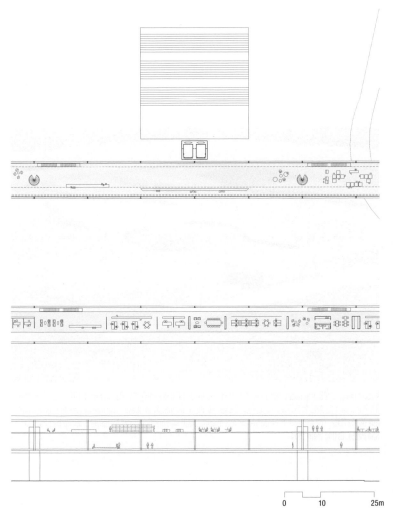

0   10   25m

Angelo Bucci, SPBR Arquitetos, Museu de Arte Moderna de São Paulo (MAM), São Paulo, Brazil, 2013,
plan and section drawings.

Angelo Bucci, SPBR arquitetos, Museu de Arte Moderna de São Paulo (MAM), São Paulo, Brazil, 2013, model for the 33º Panorama da Arte Brasileira exhibition "Unique Forms of Continuity in Space," curated by Lisette Lagnado and Ana Maria Maia. The museum is conceived as a continuous wall surrounding Oscar Niemeyer's Ibirapuera Park in São Paulo, dating from 1954.

Angelo Bucci, SPBR Arquitetos, Museu de Arte Moderna de São Paulo (MAM), São Paulo, Brazil, 2013, rendering with Niemeyer's Palácio das Exposições.

Angelo Bucci, SPBR Arquitetos, Museu de Arte Moderna de São Paulo (MAM), São Paulo, Brazil, 2013, aerial view.

Angelo Bucci, SPBR Arquitetos, Museu de Arte Moderna de São Paulo (MAM), São Paulo, Brazil, 2013.

Angelo Bucci, SPBR Arquitetos, Museu de Arte Moderna de São Paulo (MAM), São Paulo, Brazil, 2013

Angelo Bucci, SPBR Arquitetos, Museu de Arte Moderna de São Paulo (MAM), São Paulo, Brazil, 2013.

On Ground

MAM was founded in 1948 by Cicillo Matarazzo
in São Paulo's downtown. At the same time,
a parallel project in the Ibirapuera Park was
being developed by Oscar Niemeyer and Roberto
Burle Marx, which would be inaugurated in
1954 in celebration of the fourth centenary
of the city.

In 1959, for the 5th Art Biennial of São Paulo,
Lina Bo Bardi proposed the exhibition enti-
tled "Bahia." The temporary pavilion for that
exhibition occupied 400 square meters under
the Ibirapuera canopy. After the exhibition,
instead of freeing the canopy, the pavilion
remained as warehouse for the Biennial.

By the early sixties, under an institutional
crisis, MAM was dissolved and its collection
was transferred to the Contemporary Art Museum
of the University of São Paulo.

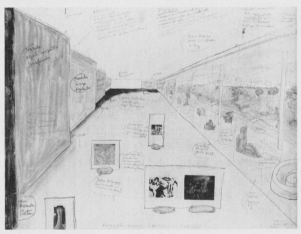

Lina Bo Bardi, sketch for MAM Pavilion, São Paulo, Brazil, 1959.

In 1969, six years after its dissolution, MAM was resurrected through an exhibition, the first Panorama of Brazilian Art, held in Lina Bo Bardi's pavilion. At that moment MAM and Ibirapuera Park ceased to exist in parallel and became linked. Since then, MAM has operated under the Ibirapuera canopy. In 1982, Lina Bo Bardi, Andre Vainer, and Marcelo Ferraz were brought back to remodel and to enlarge the 900-square-meter pavilion, now considered the official location of MAM.

The interaction of these institutions has been fraught with controversy. Thus the question brought by Lisette Lagnado and Ana Maria Maia for the 33° Panorama has been voiced before and remains a pertinent question for both institutions since 1969. A proper response to the prompt requires more than siding with either Lina Bo Bardi or Oscar Niemeyer. It is not enough to choose MAM or Ibirapuera Park. Rather, it is imperative to take into account the history of both institutions, including their conflictive coexistence, to be able to overcome a few apparent oppositions: Niemeyer and Bo Bardi, museum and canopy, park and city.

Our proposal intended to show that the controversial coexistence between MAM and Ibirapuera Park was actually fruitful, that the polemical debate between Lina Bo Bardi and Oscar Niemeyer enriches our architectural culture. The New MAM for São Paulo takes the question brought by the curators and honors the precedents to show how we could set up the museum, the park, and the city in a unique way, something impossible elsewhere in the world. Just imagine a museum

that holds in its permanent collection gardens
by Burle Marx and buildings by Oscar Niemeyer.

In its current position, the existing MAM is
not visible in an aerial view; it is hidden
underneath the canopy. In this view one can
see, in the middle of the park designed by
Burle Marx, the trace of Oscar Niemeyer high-
lighting the canopy lines. Pure geometric
figures for the five buildings, with their
defined programs of activities, contrast the
sinuous shape of the canopy and its unpro-
grammed spaces. The geometric rigor that guides
Niemeyer's original ensemble is not so obvious.
Still in aerial view, one can see former areas
of park that were split, donated, or otherwise
reoccupied. The Ibirapuera has lost
some pieces of its original scheme.   ← figs. 017 & 018

Against the erasure of these details, we wanted
to consider the new MAM as a device that sharp-
ens our perception of the city. Why? This is
a museum whose collection is revealed in such
a way that what it holds inside reverberates
outside, and the outside context invades its
interior. An everything museum. For whom? This
is a museum whose exhibition is revealed not
only to its visitors but also to people walking through the park or passing by in a car on
those avenues. An everyone museum.

Four identical prisms each measuring 750 meters
by 10 meters by 10 meters are arranged to make
a square in plan, encompassing the park and its
integral buildings. The 10 meter by 10 meter
cross section expands in all directions with
glazing and with transparent floors, offering a

window to the park and vice-versa. The façades
are protected by louvers in order to calibrate
the sunlight according to orientation and exhi-
bitions. In this way the New MAM overcomes
the Ibirapuera Park boundaries and
recovers its lost extension.   ← figs. 019, 020, & 021

The New MAM is a building that encompasses
different scales of time, a construction that
exists on an architectural and an urban scale.
It is a building that cannot be read entirely
in a single glance, but which is more clearly
understood through its history and meaning.

LUGANO

Andrea Pedrazzini, a structural engineer who
practices in Lugano, Switzerland, invited me
to design an apartment building in the city in
2008. The project had a precedent, a proposal
designed by the architects Nicola Baserga and
Christian Mozzetti. That previous study was
invaluable in giving us insight into Lugano's
land use regulations as well as the work of
building in a Swiss context, and informed
early design concepts as well. During the whole
development of the project and construction
I had Baserga and Mozzetti as local partners,
a quite supportive collaboration—besides, of
course, Andrea Pedrazzini and his partners,
who were in charge of the structural engineering, project management, and construction work
supervision. The team I had in Lugano was
quite remarkable for its skill and capacity,
and more than that for its generosity, sensi-
bility, and friendship.

More and more I understood the richness of
the architectural context in Ticino. There the
current generation of architects has developed
in departure from a legacy of four notable
forebears: Luigi Snozzi, Livio Vacchini, Aure-
lio Galfetti, and Mario Botta. Their precedents
allowed for the rise of architects like Nicola
Baserga, Giacomo Guidoti, and Stefano Moor.

The irregular polygon of the site has seven
sides and measures about 1,000 square meters.
The required setbacks inscribe a smaller polygon of 330 square meters in which it was
possible to build beyond three meters above
ground level. Within that inner figure we could
only have 230 square meters per floor, considering the maximum height allowed (six floors)
and the building program. The geometry of the
slabs has two centers supporting two cores of
activity. On the first three floors the slabs
correspond to two separate small apartments,
and for the three upper floors, they organize
to two different programs in one
large apartment.   → fig. 022

These two cores are supported by a corresponding
concrete wall, which forms a T-shape with the
ceiling to receive both vertical and horizontal
loads. Extra-thin columns, placed on the extreme
north end of the scheme, free the slab geometry
from the limits of the two struc-
tural walls. This also liberates the   → fig. 023
slabs of unnecessary beams. There-
fore, the slab plane has no clearly readable
direction. As a result, the rigorous geometry of
walls and columns cannot be easily
apprehended on the interior.   → fig. 024

Each façade is either an opaque plane made
with wood panels or a transparent one made with
glazed panels. The opaque plane always meets a
transparent one. From the inside, one always
has a view outside, and from the exterior the
building volume seems like it is constructed
without solids and only by planes.

The ground level is an open passage that shares
two different programs—housing and office. The
office space is set slightly into the ground in
the middle of the garden. Partly submerged and
protected by the two structural reinforced concrete walls, the space is quite discrete. The
curiously truncated height of the ground level
as seen from the exterior brings some vitality
to a peripheral corner of the site.
At this level, the residential pro- → fig. 025
gram is only announced by a small
abstract prism, the elevator hall, the size and
detailing of which were carefully calibrated to
limit its impact on the space.

There are two floors underground for parking
and for storage. The parking garage covers the
entire available area of the site, about 650
square meters, and it is shallow enough to
allow us to preserve a historic retaining wall
at Pico Street. The ambience of the parking
level feels as though it is on the
surface of the earth, not below it. → fig. 026

Back above ground, the façade panels were designed to achieve the Swiss standard for energy
consumption, the "Minergie." The wood panel
exterior is ventilated and assembled on a
frame which holds successive layers of thermal

insulation, a vapor barrier, and an inside dry-
wall panel. The glazing has triple glass panels
on aluminum frame, and the south and west glass
façades are shaded by retractable
aluminum louvers. Thermal losses → fig. 027
are also drastically reduced by a
mechanical system of independently controlled
ventilation in each apartment. Heating and
cooling needs are reduced by four geothermal
loops that burrow 225 meters into the earth.

THE OPPOSITE OF GLOBAL ACTION

I tend to consider my experience in Lugano as
the opposite of what is called globalization.
Instead of suppressing any possibility for
a local practice and vocabulary, it means an
action to enlarge our field of possibility.
This cultural turn creates possibility from the
potential of both Brazilian and Swiss contexts.

In a way it is not easy to consider the other's
constraints. From eyes trained in Europe looking at some Brazilian projects, we often hear
about how permissive the climatic conditions
in the tropics are, or how easy it would be to
work in a context were the rules are so relaxed.
They tend to see as a freedom what we experience as precariousness. In the opposite way,
it is common to hear from a Brazilian architect about how easy it would be to work with
a European budget. We tend to see freedom in
what they experience as sometimes compromised
commitments.

The change of context can show more clearly
what is less perceptible in a familiar working
environment. My Brazilian colleagues used to
ask how I could deal with all the rules and
norms that regulate construction in Switzerland. But now I can show you this project and
point to several features I was able to explore
in Switzerland, things that would not be per-
mitted in Brazil. A wood façade for a six-story
building, floor-to-ceiling glazing, an outside
egress staircase, a single lift for a building—
none of these would be allowed by our code.
Even a common rooftop garden wouldn't be possible due to a crazy rule imposed by
the São Paulo real estate market.   → fig. 028

But there are also some design opportunities
that only present themselves once we merge
cultural backgrounds. One example is the open
ground level. It is true that modern architecture in Brazil found a fruitful field in which
to develop a remarkable repertoire of pilotis
and open spaces, mostly in the 1950s and 1960s.
However, more recently, possibilities to pro-
pose such spaces are more and more scarce due
to social and safety concerns and to the often
paranoid approach to those issues. Maybe this
is the best example that emerged from fusing
Brazilian and Swiss perspectives and contexts,
this open ground. Of course it is not a new
invention in architectural language, but it is
a possibility that we were able to discern and
realize. Here the ground is an international
meeting point.

Angelo Bucci, SPBR Arquitetos, Apartment Building in Lugano, Switzerland, 2010.

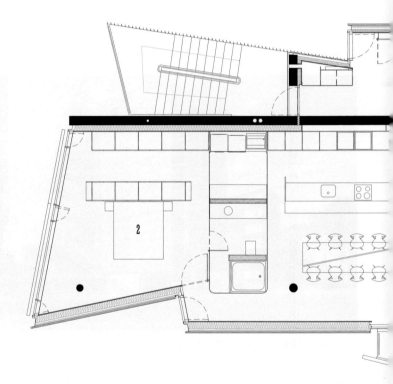

023

1. Living Room
2. Master Bedroom
3. Children's Living Room
4. Bedrooms

Angelo Bucci, SPBR Arquitetos, Apartment Building in Lugano, Switzerland, 2010, typical floor plan drawing.

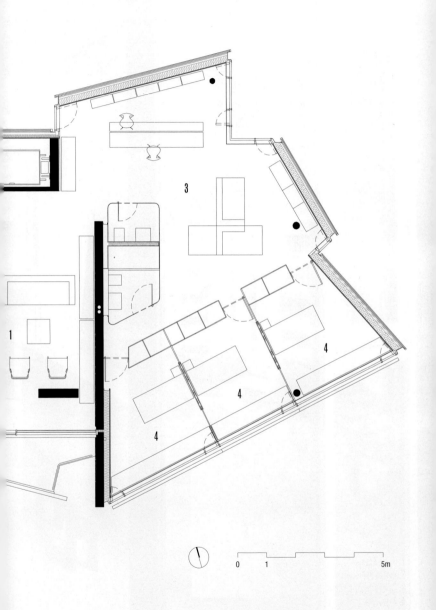

1

3

4

4

4

4

0   1   5m

Angelo Bucci, SPBR Arquitetos, Apartment Building in Lugano, Switzerland, 2010, interior, looking out.

Angelo Bucci, SPBR Arquitetos, Apartment Building in Lugano, Switzerland, 2010, suspended entry level at grade.

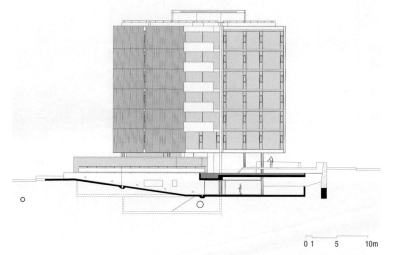

Angelo Bucci, SPBR Arquitetos, Apartment Building in Lugano, Switzerland, 2010, section showing entry level with parking beneath.

Angelo Bucci, SPBR Arquitetos, Apartment Building in Lugano, Switzerland, 2010, entry level with screened access stair.

Angelo Bucci, SPBR Arquitetos, Apartment Building in Lugano, Switzerland, 2010, roof terrace.

"The dissolution of the building, contrary to what one might suppose, heightens its architectonic interest and its discursive power because it allows the building to speak through its urban surroundings."

THE DISSOLUTION OF BUILDINGS
Angelo Bucci

São Paulo, aerial view of the city center showing the various bridges that cross over the Anhangabaú Valley.

I

A boy with wrinkled clothes glides through an abandoned industrial area full of old warehouses and depots, all empty, toward a lowland and its pollution-clouded river.

He balances himself on a railway car moving at sixty kilometers per hour; he is on top of a freight train approaching the city center from the eastern periphery. The ocean of this surfer is above his head, made from a fluid of wires and cables, the waves of which come from the sky and give rhythm to the raising and lowering of his torso as if they were blows. Railroad surfing is not a sport but an exercise in the military understanding of the term—survival conditioning in an environment of war. The surprising lightness of this surfer is not the physical lightness of velocity and dexterity, but rather the lightness of balance upon an immense and dynamic mass. Subverting the dominant force that infrastructure exerts upon bodies in the city, he flies.

This flight outlines our journey. The image of the train surfer is provocative because it demonstrates the possibility of overcoming, which is the purpose of this study. Such possibility is evident when it is expressed without the need for preconditions. This kind of possibility transforms inherent weaknesses into resources, resources for accomplishing real, human, meaningful life. In this way, the surfer is a survivor.

The hypothesis that drives the following architectural tour d'horizon is that all architectural projects are built from elements latent in the city, and that even as these elements—from elevator cars to the people within them—are mobilized in specific structures they remain part of the greater urban fabric. The city, in other words, informs the activity of the architect. Using São Paulo as a case study, this text attempts to understand how the city inflects our ways of thinking about and operating in and on architecture.

Our experience of the city participates in our imagination of any architectural space, and the "elements" that define this experience reveal themselves through their physical materialization. In this state, they are already condensed—a superimposition of hard facts that compose the urban environment. But this brute physicality also belies the more transitory and subjective forms of perception that the city allows. Therefore, the approaches proposed in this text are designed to shed light upon distinct aspects of a common reality—the perceivable world that influences the perception of the architect.

What is the object of study?

It is not the city. For the architect, the city is simultaneously the raw material of architecture and a thing in flux that demands intervention. It is a target for transformative architectural action, and it is the context in which those actions operate. The activity of the architect oscillates between these poles. It is not architectural intervention, nor the city, nor even the built projects that constitute the city that are the object of this study. The city is not treated as a problem to be solved, as something for which there is a right answer. Rather, the city is described as an environment or arrangement in which its own buildings dissolve.

As such, this analysis of the city moves away from technical representation such as plans and instead suggests images, impressions imprinted in the mind. It is through such impressions that buildings dissolve into the environment of the city; and our understanding of them moves away from an idea of isolated, discrete forms and instead moves toward an understanding of buildings as parts within a whole. In other words, the object of investigation here is not the city, but the urban environment. Using diverse approaches, we can sketch something in constant transformation—the activity of an architect whose imagination is informed by the current urban milieu when thinking and operating in architecture.

We must also not lose sight of the unbuilt facts that shape the built environment. This is how violence, for instance, transforms our deepest fears into walls. They are literally and solidly built, yet we barely see them. Crystallized forms of violence in the construction of urban space, fused into the artifacts that sustain our everyday existence, influence our patterns of behavior and the way we relate to the urban environment. Violence imperceptibly permeates customs and habits, our way of life in the city. In São Paulo, violent action is commonplace. Breaking down the historical social contract between citizens and city government, violence imprints itself on the physical landscape through the afterimages of destruction and tactics of fortification and security while shaping how we move through and inhabit public and private space. Violence pervades space in formal, technical, and symbolic ways, to borrow from the classifications suggested by the eminent Brazilian geographer Milton Santos in his book *A Natureza do Espaço* (The Nature of Space), which provides a preliminary structure for the approaches proposed here.[1]

Through a reversal of values—and of reason itself—violence becomes a foundation upon which we operate and upon which we build. It establishes parameters that in turn are folded into the rules of conduct that guide our actions in urban space.

This thinking emanates from a world molded by hegemony, a system that regulates the city at the expense of its human dimension. This reversal throws the very idea of the city as an institution into crisis. The institutional understanding of the city relies on an ethical agreement between its inhabitants that is expressed in the rules that govern our coexistence. As the social contract gradually erodes, this agreement ceases to prevail. A lack of social contract and lack of rules characterize the void through which urban violence spreads. The crisis of the idea of the city puts the purpose of architecture into crisis as well. The latter is felt on two interrelated fronts: professional practice and education. In professional practice, this occurs because the crisis of the idea of city leads to less optimism about architecture and consequently less demand for it; the very environment in which architecture operates has become potentially pernicious. The crisis within the practice of architecture has been expressed by a single question: How can projects be proposed in a city that seems to have lost its meaning?[2]

The crisis in architectural education arises when it becomes difficult to imagine safe public (and even private) spaces. These, after all, are the physical interiors that incubate productive images of the city and the exterior environments that facilitate interaction and coexistence. How can architectural education be developed when the infrastructure that supports architectural thinking seems to have ceased to exist? To what extent does violence, when acting as a norm in the urban environment, influence the way we conceptualize the city, even before we form a response to it?

II   FOUR OPERATIONS:
HOW TO PASS THROUGH WALLS

I put a picture up on a wall. Then I forget there is a wall. I no longer know what there is behind this wall, I no longer know there is a wall, I no longer know this wall is a wall, I no longer know what a wall is. I no longer know that in my apartment there are walls, and that if there weren't any walls, there would be no apartment. The wall is no longer what delimits and defines the place where I live, that which separates it from other places where other people live; it is nothing more than a support for the picture. But I also forget the picture, I no longer look at it, I no longer know how to look at it. I have put the picture on the wall so as to forget there was a wall, but in forgetting the wall, I forget the picture, too. There are pictures because there are walls. We have to be able to forget these walls, and we have found no better way to do that than with pictures. Pictures efface walls. But walls kill pictures. So we are continually exchanging one for the other, either the wall or the picture, to be forever putting other pictures up on the walls, or else constantly moving the picture from one wall to another.

My hypothesis here is that poetic images are capable of sustaining a safe passage through walls. For this I present four images created during a journey through central São Paulo. They can be understood as four imaginary performances. Their purpose is to sustain the proposition of projects. In each case the practical character or imagination of the architect prevails over the architectonic or constructive elements. Four images that sustain projective operations in the urban environment are:

— To Look Out (to overcome the obstructed view)

— To Cross (to shift levels in the "vertical city")

— To Invade (from the flatland to the river basin)

— To Infiltrate (from the river basin beneath the flatland)

These images are substitutions or reconstructions, both less than what is offered by the city and less than what the city denies its inhabitants. These operations are infused into the voids of the urban imaginary. Here the "absence" assumes a motor function and adds meaning to the process of projective imagination. In this case the image is also an action.

For my approach proposed here (and to borrow from Rafael Iglesia), "image" is a verb and not a noun.[3] Therefore, to look, to cross, to invade, and to infiltrate are four methods of image-making, actions which sustain four operations.

1   To Look Out (to overcome the obstructed view)

The railroad and the bridge, two typologies particularly present in São Paulo, constitute a "street" that is completely constructed and mechanized. Together they express the installations and institutions that support the existence of the city. They are arranged on the horizontal plane as public infrastructure. Systems of public transport—trams, metro, and even buses—are to some extent related to the railroad in the same way as the configuration of public infrastructure is related to the street grid, whether in a mechanical sense or in its obedience to the street arrangement. Thus these public programs or infrastructures are typically connected to the horizontal plane, which defines the "floor" of the city.

The horizontal plane lies close to the surface of the planet. Made by a multiplicity of axes, it tends to weave a mesh that is increasingly overlapped and closed. As such it presents itself as a plane, and in most cities it manifests itself as a kind of flatness. In São Paulo, however, this shifting horizontal plane is quite thick. Its thickness derives from the geography of the city when it was first settled. It is about 20 meters or 6 stories high. Bridges have belted this uncommon thickness. Yet the plane grows above and below this surface, taking on more and more thickness. In São Paulo, geography transformed the bridge into one single urban landscape.

The force of the shifting horizontal plane and its thickness dissolves the two vertical axes on either side of São Paulo's river valley. Yet the extensions of its horizontal axes dissolve the city so that it merges into other cities, regions, and countries. The entire infrastructure, which allows the "operation" of the city, is included in this horizontal plane. The thickness of the plane is greater than what is contained at its surface: It grows into the earth, underground and above, but it is always obedient to the horizontal plane of the planet's surface.

Railways, roads, waterways, or tubes, electrical cables, fiber optics, air routes, and satellite orbits—all are superimposed meshes and part of the same horizontal plane defined by the ground. The city is one particular moment in this mesh where the density increases. In the city the plane tends toward consistency. The scale of this plane is planetary, linked to the environment upon which all cities are sited and dependent for air, water, and earth—everything produced by these primordial elements. This scale is present in the Roman aqueducts, in the cisterns of Istanbul, and in every merchant ship ever launched into the sea. Each man walking on a path of compacted dirt has, potentially, this same planetary monumentality. Despite the planetary origin of the horizontal plane, in São Paulo it is redefined by the current context.

The lookout is a characteristic of the geography of São Paulo's horizontal plane—the flatland 20 meters above the Tamanduateí Valley, where the city was first settled as a Jesuit village five centuries ago. It was a walled settlement, introverted. The hill served as a barrier of defense and the lookout as a means to keep watch. The Tamanduateí, when viewed in cross section, seems asymmetrical. The slope that marks the end of the historic hill, to its left edge, does not reemerge on the right bank where the river basin loosely extends. For this reason, when you look from the right edge of the valley to the hill, the magnificence of the slope stands out; and in the opposite direction, from the top of the plateau, the lookout condition is accentuated by the extension of the view.

The city now appears to have already lost the link to the original historic conditions that made it a walled settlement. Buildings today are constructed to maintain the same relationship with the landscape. They turn themselves to the historical core with their backs to the east, their backs to the view, and their backs to the river basin. Even now buildings are built for reasons that have been lost for centuries. To look out, in this case, does not denote a contemplative gaze; on the contrary, to look out is to do so indicatively, like a gesture pointing to where the other three images of action will be deployed between the city divided into two territories—the river basin and the flatland.

To reclaim the lookout for a street like Boa Vista— paradoxically laid out and built up to block its "good view" (the road runs alongside the plateau's rim, hence its name)—does not require the undoing of the buildings that are constructed there. It is enough to open, even partially, the ground floors of those buildings, which are at an elevation of 745 meters. This operation ruptures the division between parcels (at least with regard to the relationship of use) of the horizontal plane at the street level of the "upper city."[4]

The geographical conditions that mark Rua Boa Vista and the walling off of its lookout by buildings are two conditions that occur in other areas as well—Rua São Bento, Libero Badaró, Xavier de Toledo, Avanhandava, and Verguei rua Monte Alegre, to name a few. They are the result of an automatic repetition of procedures rooted in our culture of exclusion, where marginalized populations are pushed to the slopes beneath the plateau.[5]

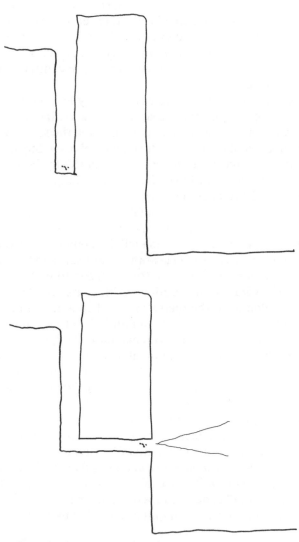

Blind lookout (above) and reclaimed lookout (below).

2   To Cross (to shift levels in the "vertical city")

Vertical buildings have programs or infrastructures that are typically private. In cross section, it is clear that these programs are organized on a vertical axis defined by the elevator and skyscraper. The elevator and skyscraper support these activities and permit the existence of another dimension accessible from the horizontal plane and the ground. However, even as a description, this analysis is excessively schematic. It does not cover, and as such does not sufficiently expose, the intricate connections between horizontal and vertical, and between public and private.

São Paulo is a city of many vertical axes all attempting to escape the planet. Each of these axes is isolated to itself. Together they can compose fragments of planes, yet they always

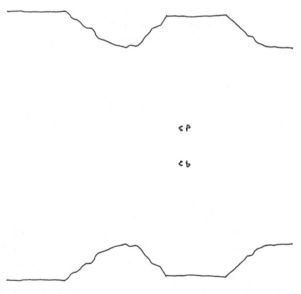

São Paulo and Rio de Janeiro seen in transverse section from the point of view of social exclusion. In Rio those outcast were pushed to the hills above, while in São Paulo those outcast were relegated to the slopes below.

tend toward the isolation of their orientation, producing voids in the pursuit of height. While the vertical axes in São Paulo accumulate, they cluster without merging. The sheer quantity of vertical axes undermines the singularity of each, so that a single value is imposed to the resulting whole. But these opposing axes aren't so easily separable. The vertical axis of the city carries, like an inverted volcano, the vitality of the shifting horizontal plane to higher and more isolated points. Part of the infrastructure present in the shifting horizontal plane is vertical, like elevators. These axial discontinuities and integrations also echo the city's conflation of public and private spaces. Because the city is contained within the buildings, the buildings will dissolve to compose the environment of the city as people ebb and flow within them. In this dissolution there are no substitutions, not one of the parts gives way to the other. In the city, the two dimensions superimpose and coexist so that both are always present as interior and exterior. But because of dissolution the two terms gain some imprecision; the classification of public and private—with "semi" this and "semi" that—becomes excessively generic.

Rua 25 de Março and Rua Boa Vista embody the two divided cities of São Paulo—"upper" and "lower," two territories of opposite elevations borne of their respective domain.

The view from the lookout indicates the desired direction of the operations; the shift of level is meant to connect the low river basin and the terra firma flatland previously disconnected by the development of the "vertical city" at these different elevation levels. This image realizes, over the 20 meters that make up the particular thickness of the "floor" of central São Paulo, what looking out only evokes.

It is worth remembering that the possibility of vertical superimposition in order to increase the "floor" of the city is especially relevant in an urban center that has suffered a brutal increase in density.[6] The city that opened the first Viaduto do Chá in 1892 had 40,000 inhabitants. At the inauguration of the new viaduct in 1938, the population had reached 1.5 million. Today that number approximates the number of people who traverse the

viaduct daily.[7] To realize a vertical city, to open up and reunite the divided city, will consolidate its history and celebrate its unique and previously hidden characteristic in
its center, that is, its particularly thick "floor." ← p. 68

3   To Invade (from the flatland to the river basin)

The image of the aerial invasion is derived from possible spatial relationships between the terra firma flatland and the river basin. It departs from a contradiction and resists the impulse to resolve that contradiction. Aziz Ab'Saber describes São Paulo as a city that leaps from hill to hill. His description evokes a lofted city, as well the passage over bridges and through viaducts that have been fundamental since the plateau of São Paulo was first settled. From its initial outcropping, the city grew above the river basin to conquer new plateaus. The meaning of this beginning of São Paulo was embodied in the act of crossing; this is evident in the viaducts and roads that still serve the old city. The river basins have systematically received the people of the excluded territories. The current westward expansion of the formal city in the direction of the ridge, as opposed to eastward toward the basin (where there were, historically, factories, workers, and immigrants), continues this original segregation. The opposition between plateau and river basin is integral to this aerial invasion, and the existing built structures that could articulate this "symbolic inversion" are vast.

The purpose of this image is to invade, to invade in order to make this vast existing urban infrastructure begin to express opposing values. Invading in this case is the opposite of crossing. To cross is to avoid, to deny. Its opposite is to invade, to merge, to understand. The idea is that those 20 vertical meters, which served to segregate the formal city and the informal city, are now 20 meters of thickness in a single city.

4   To Infiltrate (from the river basin beneath the flatland)

A valley carved by the rushing water of a small creek divides the plateau and creates an isolated hill where the historic nucleus of the city was settled. This "enclosure," open to the sky, is a portion of the floodplain imprisoned between two halves of the terra firma flatland.

The floodplain corresponds to its most shallow level, the area of the upper city (an invasion beneath the plateau). It is like descending into the earth only to be surprised by the light, because there, at the city's center, the flatland pulls up the "floor" to reencounter the second floor, 20 meters underground and lit with sunshine.

Subterranean infiltration performs an inverse operation and complements aerial invasion. Together, they integrate with our crossing and looking out. All four operations—to look, to cross, to invade, and to infiltrate—work simultaneously to reconcile two divided territories. What, after all, do these operations sustain? The possibility to pass through those walls, physical and otherwise, that restrict the activity of the architect. These operations, from the standpoint of spatial arrangements, will be able to unfold in architectural projects. What do those walls deny us? Mobility, interactivity, freedom, and the fullest experience of the city, the ability to truly see the urban environment. The four images that demonstrate these operations, together and simultaneously, allow for the aesthetic pleasure of architectonic possibilities to be realized in the unusual thickness of São Paulo's ground level, its floor. The walls are no longer noticeable when these images are overlaid and the two divided territories are spatially reconciled.

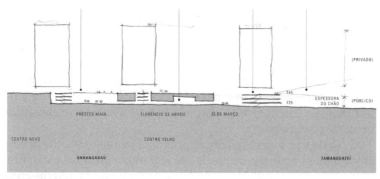

Four operations.

III

A cross section through central São Paulo reveals both the topography and the architecture of the city. The drawing identifies four operations that open up possible architectural projects. This sketch may start the first step in a process that will culminate in the ideas and diagrams used to construct future buildings. I consider these four images and operations to be generative and therefore healthy and healing. The design projects that they may lead to confer on them a real human meaning; therefore, as operations, they do not end. The operations are practical responses intended as provocations, pushing the imagination of the architect within the urban environment. They are the architect's way of reacting to the experience of the city. In the city, buildings present themselves as dissolved. As isolated objects they are not capable of complete expression because the meaning of each one alone cannot be divorced from the whole urban assemblage into which they have dissipated. These indefinite boundaries mark the way the urban environment presents itself to the perceptive process of the architect. This is why it is so important to guide action, to open up ways of seeing instead of dictating what it is we have seen.

The dissolution of the building, contrary to what one might suppose, heightens its architectonic interest and its discursive power because it allows the building to speak through its urban surroundings. Through dissolution, the seeming disarray of the city's fabric is suddenly distilled by new points of view and precise lines of sight. Because of this, it is possible to intervene in an urban area to make what was already there more lucid and to express open, inclusive values in opposition to the values that have historically shaped the city. The new proposition produces a new whole.

To do this I changed my approach. I began to see the urban environment from the inside, to see in it its constitutive elements, in search of a something already there that could undo the conditions that gave rise to it. I see two elements. They correspond to the way we learn to guide ourselves in the world: horizontal and vertical, floor and zenith, the extension of the planet that keeps us and the direction of outer space into which we escape. The relationships between built things and people, between the inside and the outside.

The Dissolution of Buildings

1   Milton Santos, *A Natureza do Esparo* (São Paulo: Hucitec, 1997).

2   This formulation was made by Dr. Luis Antonio Jorge during a qualification review of this research at FAU, University of São Paulo, November 22, 2004.

3   Rafael Iglesia, an architect from Argentina, uses this distinction when he refers to architecture. It is a verb and not a noun.

4   There have been examples of this rupture in division: the gallery lots of the 1950s in Centro Novo and, today, the renovation of the FIESP building; Paulo Mendes da Rocha's 1996 project is a paradigmatic case.

5   This condition of the lookout was explored by architect Lina Bo Bardi in her conception of the Museu de Arte de São Paulo, which produced a building that is the only exception to the walled Avenida Paulista.

6   It is worth noting that the large difference between the Centro of the 1950s and its degradation today is the density of people (bringing a specialization of programs that comes with another factor for degradation); the architecture that characterized the elegant Centro is practically the same architecture that today is associated with degradation.

7   According to a report in the *Gazeta Mercantil* in 1994, 1.5 million people and 580 vehicles per hour passed over the viaduct.

"The practice of architecture in Brazil has never been entirely divorced from radical politics."

ANGELO BUCCI AND THE PAULISTA MODERN HOUSE
Kenneth Frampton

Paulo Mendes da Rocha, Butantã House in São Paulo, 1964. A private dwelling treated as though it were a semi-public domain!

Unlike the Anglo-American world where aesthetic form, philosophical reflection, and politics are seen as incompatible, in Brazil this seems not to have been the case, which surely explains why the practice of architecture in Brazil has never been entirely divorced from radical politics. In this respect, it is significant that the two most prominent father figures of the Brazilian modern movement—Oscar Niemeyer in Rio de Janeiro, and João Batista Vilanova Artigas in São Paulo—were both committed to the communist cause throughout their lives, however much their practices may have differed from each other's.

Artigas's involvement with the creation of the Faculty of Architecture and Urban Design at the University of São Paulo (FAU USP) over the years 1960–65, both as the architect of the building and the initiator of the curriculum, may be fairly compared to Walter Gropius's creation of the Dessau Bauhaus in 1925 and Max Bill's reformation of the Bauhaus through the Hochschule für Gestaltung founded in Ulm in 1955. In all three instances we have a significant architect not only designing the building but also inventing the pedagogical program. Although Angelo Bucci, who graduated from FAU in 1987, was never a student of Artigas's, the building itself, along with the continuity of the curriculum, was enough to leave him with the feeling that he had indeed been a direct pupil of Artigas. As Bucci remarked in his lecture to the school:

> This building stands as a kind of monument to this Paulista legacy, but more than the veneration of some remarkable professors, in true Grecian fashion, the history of the school of architecture was marked from the beginning by tragedy. Just one month after its inauguration, under the military dictatorship, Vilanova Artigas was persecuted and expelled from the school. Artigas would be back twelve years later, in 1981, unfortunately for a very short period before his death in 1985. Even after the political situation changed, the fact he and some other professors had been brought back didn't mean the damage produced during those years had been overcome. Amnesty aside, the powers installed

at the university during the dictatorship
would last for decades after that. ← pp. 35–36

However, as Bucci informs us, the building was didactic in
itself; its rhythmically rational 2.75-meter module served as a
normative scale, making the students constantly aware of the
dimensions by which it was ordered. As Bucci notes, it was 110
meters long and 66 meters wide, with columns at every 11 or 22
meters and with varying floor-to-ceiling heights ranging from
3.4 meters to 16.8 meters. In addition to this mute daily demonstration of a harmonic/tectonic order, Bucci acknowledges the
distinguished professors that taught there during his time as
a student, and he gives particular credit to two figures, Flávio
Motta and Paulo Mendes da Rocha. Like Artigas, Mendes da
Rocha was dismissed from the school by the military junta, but
with the restoration of democracy he would go on to become
one of the most inspiring practitioners for the architects of
Bucci's generation.

Like the Carioca School of Niemeyer and Lucio Costa, which
involved the work of the brilliant engineer Emílio Baumgart,
the Paulista School of Artigas and Mendes da Rocha was predicated on a vital culture of reinforced concrete construction
that bordered on civil engineering in terms of both its scale
and its tectonic expressivity. What is particularly telling about
this tradition is that this aesthetic and technical capacity was
combined with an implicitly radical social agenda. This libera-
tive approach, somewhat paradoxically, led to a reformulation
of the middle class dwelling, in such a way as to transform the
traditional bourgeois home into a space of public appearance.
As Pedro Fiori Arantes put it in his 2004 essay "Reinventing
the Building Site":

> Paradoxically, this project fitted into the political per-
> spective of the Brazilian Communist Party, for whom the
> bourgeois-democratic revolution led not by the proletariat
> but the middle-classes was a necessary historic step. The
> act of imagining a reformed bourgeois home was therefore

considered a strategic act. Attempts to solve working-class housing, on the other hand, were considered at that time to be reactionary and better postponed—a point of view backed by a somewhat narrow reading of Friedrich Engel's *The Housing Question* (1872), according to which the provision of housing would only diminish the revolutionary impetus of the working class.[1]

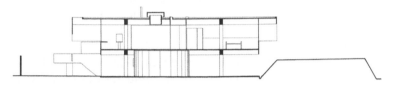

Paulo Mendes da Rocha, Butantã House in São Paulo, 1964, section drawing.

The Paulista modern house as a magically suspended semi-public realm was first formulated in the open plan of Mendes da Rocha's own house in the suburb of Butantã of 1964–66, with its concrete roofs and floors carried on exposed, cantilevered, rough-cast reinforced concrete beams which deliver their final load to the ground via the minimal structure of four concrete piers, precisely disposed in relation to the square plan of the house. Apart from the bril- ← p. 86 liant economy of this statical invention, the key to the remarkable originality of this work is the way in which it brings together topography, structure, vegetation, and light. No one has written more perceptively about this exceptional synthesis than Annette Spiro in her 2002 study on the work of Mendes da Rocha:

> The roof is pulled down like a large hat...the two-sided solid eaves allows only indirect light into the space from one side, additionally softened by large plants. A sense of twilight arises that is unexpectedly and sharply brightened in the building's depth by skylights...The third source of light is the highly unusual light that enters into the space from below...The green, earthly light allows the roof to

float and establishes a highly unusual relationship with the ground for a building on pilotis...A new and unusual notion concerning its social use lies at the core of this house. 'This is the place where one can distinguish between that which we want to call 'personal space' and 'non-personal space.' This is space as a societal project. Here the description of a 'rationalized slum becomes clear, where every person accepts the presence of the other, without solid walls but rather with new and desirable conditions of human respect.' What the philosopher and art historian Flávio Motta touches upon here is a social model which has little to do with the notion of the bourgeoisie residence...His buildings do not want to be objects on view. In his mind, they are tools with which to comprehend and question the world.[2]

Paulo Mendes da Rocha, Antonio Gerassi House in São Paulo, 1988.

This concept of a dwelling, hovering above a bermed earthwork, was what Angelo Bucci and his partners in MMBB Arquitetos, namely Fernando de Mello Franco, Marta Moreira, and Milton Braga, took as their mutual point of departure in the first instance from the Butantã House and, in the second, from Mendes's even more urbane Antonio Gerassi House of 1988, where a single, open, unshielded floor is directly visible from the outside.

A synthesis of the ideas embodied in these houses first appears in the Mariante House, which was built to their designs in 2002, in the Aldeia da Serra district of São Paulo. As in the Butantã House, the whole thing is predicated in section on a bermed earthwork with the parking beneath, enabling one to enter into the suspended living floor from a straight, steel stair hanging down to access the "green" parking space beneath at grade. In this instance, the square plan comprises a U-shaped living space complemented by a bedroom wing running along the fourth side of the square. The whole once again is carried on four columns, and the architects' awareness of the prominence of this concept is evident from their 2004 description of the house:

> This concrete and glass house in the suburbs of São Paulo is a contemporary reinterpretation of the Paulista modernism of the 1960s. Situated on a long, steeply sloping site with an 8-meter fall, each of the three levels connects to the ground, the upper two by the means of bridges.

> Entrance to the house is either from below or more spectacularly from above, over the bridge, across the roof and down through the central staircase. The roof is a pond, which maintains the water tightness of the concrete. The living area is on the first floor *piano nobile* and is wrapped around the open staircase core with the bedrooms set to one side. In the tradition of Paulista modernism, the house is supported on four columns, here set inside and the floor and roof slabs cantilevered from them...The interior is enclosed on all four sides by floor to ceiling glass attached without any frame being visible from inside...screens at the sides of the house protecting the interior from sunlight are made out of composite wood and cement panels...

With this work, MMBB, with whom Mendes da Rocha had collaborated on many occasions, elected to distance themselves somewhat from his heroic *béton brut* approach by opting for a more refined concrete finish combined with a crowning display of a light-weight tubular steel passarelle and access stair. One may see this in retrospect as the initial crystallization of Bucci's independent imagination, which he will advance further in his Ubatuba House and an unusual weekend house that he recently completed on a relatively dense urban site in São Paulo. These are two domestic essays which one may now recognize as being symptomatic of Bucci's manner—above all, his propensity for placing the swimming pool at the highest possible level, as in the Mariante House.

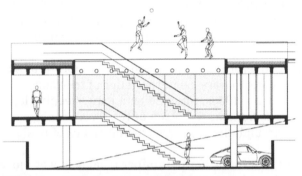

MMBB Arquitectos, Mariante House in São Paulo, 2002, section drawing.

MMBB Arquitectos, Mariante House in São Paulo, 2002. The house suspended above the grade level with pedestrian access above via an aerial passarelle.

Needless to say, such audacity depends, as always, on the brilliant Brazilian concrete tradition, calculated, in this instance, as in all of Bucci's work to date, by the talented engineer Ibsen Puleo Uvo.

The most daring gesture in Bucci's recent career is surely his Ubatuba House where the entire house sits on three cylindrical concrete columns instead of the four as per the Butantã paradigm. Here the elevated house is broken up into three cubic components comprising the living space on top and three bedroom wings on the level beneath linked by stairs and bridges to the vertical circulation, which, in this instance, is a spiral stair wrapped around a column. The whole improbable feat is achieved by suspending the house from two parallel concrete girders that are integral to the roofwork at the top of the structure.

We may think of Bucci's weekend house in São Paulo as a condensed version of the Ubatuba project, which is now axially suspended in a leftover space between two 6½-meter-high buildings set 10 meters apart. This time the elevated construction drops down onto three concrete piers from which various components cantilever out, including a longitudinal living volume and, at the very top, a lap pool and sun deck. While this was the only way to provide adequate sunlight for the swimming pool of an "in town" weekend house on a relatively narrow site enclosed by high party walls, it also provided an occasion for the creation of a vertical tropical garden, cascading down from planters at the level of the lap pool and transforming the entire lot into a vertical arboretum, now attended on a daily basis by the tropical fauna of the region. Here, as in the great Brazilian modern tradition common to both Rio and São Paulo, nature and culture are to be found inextricably mixed together.

1   Pedro Fiori Arantes, "Reinventing the Building Site" in *Brazil's Modern Architecture*, Elisabetta Andreoli and Adrian Forty, eds. (New York: Phaidon, 2004), 181–82.

2   Annette Spiro, *Paulo Mendes da Rocha: Works and Projects* (Zurich: Niggli, 2002), 17.

Image Credits & Biographies

Angelo Bucci, <u>On Ground</u>

Figs. 001-002, 004-005, and 008 courtesy of Erieta Attali

Figs. 007, 009-010, 013, 022, 024-025, and 027-028 courtesy of Nelson Kon

Figs. 017-021: rendering by Ciro Miguel, SPBR Arquitetos

P. 37 courtesy of FAU USP São Paulo

P. 39 courtesy of Nelson Kon

P. 49 courtesy of Instituto Lina Bo e P. M. Bardi

Angelo Bucci, *The Dissolution of Buildings*

P. 68 courtesy of Nelson Kon

Kenneth Frampton, *Angelo Bucci and the Paulista Modern House*

Pp. 86 and 90 courtesy of Nelson Kon

For over twenty-five years, ANGELO BUCCI has been dedicated to building design, sharing his time between academic and professional practice. These parallel activities define a special approach to his projects, in which the professional demands are understood as an engaging opportunity to research and speculate new ideas. Bucci is founder and principal of São Paulo-based SPBR Architects. He was also founder and associate of MMBB Architects from 1996 to 2002. He has taught studios at the University of São Paulo and also as a visiting professor in Argentina, Chile, Ecuador, Italy, Switzerland, and the United States.

KENNETH FRAMPTON is a renowned architectural historian and author of many seminal essays and books, including <u>Modern Architecture: A Critical History</u>. He is the Ware Professor of Architecture at the Columbia University Graduate School of Architecture, Planning and Preservation.

SERIES EDITORS
James Graham &
Caitlin Blanchfield

SERIES DESIGN
Neil Donnelly &
Stefan Thorsteinsson

VOLUME DESIGN
Neil Donnelly

COPY EDITOR
Walter Ancarrow

PRINTER
Die Keure

COLUMBIA BOOKS ON
ARCHITECTURE AND THE CITY
An imprint of The Graduate
School of Architecture,
Planning and Preservation
Columbia University
1172 Amsterdam Ave.
407 Avery Hall
New York, NY 10027

Visit our website at
arch.columbia.edu/books

Columbia Books on
Architecture and the City
are distributed by
Columbia University Press
at cup.columbia.edu

This book has been produced
through the Office of the
Dean, Amale Andraos, and
the Office of Publications.

ISBN 978-1-941332-18-4

LIBRARY OF CONGRESS
CATALOGING-IN-PUBLICATION DATA
The dissolution of buildings /
Angelo Bucci ; With an essay
by Kenneth Frampton.
        pages cm. --
(GSAPP transcripts)
  ISBN 978-1-941332-18-4
1. SPBR (Firm)
2. Architecture,
Domestic--Brazil--São
Paulo--History--20th
century. 3. Architecture,
Domestic--Brazil--São Paulo--
History--21st century. I.
Bucci, Angelo, author. II.
Frampton, Kenneth. Angelo
Bucci and the Paulista
modern house. III. Columbia
University. Graduate School of
Architecture, Planning, and
Preservation.
  NA859.S63B83 2015
  728.0981'61--dc23
2015032640